lonely planet

M

BAR CELONA

D1466045

1. FLIP

FLIP through the activity cards for morning, afternoon and evening.

MORNING

LA SAGRADA FAMÍLIA

2. MATCH

CHOOSE your perfect day by mixing and matching the cards.

AFTERNOON

MERCAT DE LA BOQUERIA

3. GO

EVERYTHING you need for your city adventure is now at your fingertips.

EVENING

TAPAS IN LA RIBERA

Spain's biggest tourist attraction is a unique, extraordinary piece of architecture. Conceived as a temple as atonement for Barcelona's sins of modernity, this giant church became Gaudí's holy mission. A work in progress for more than a century, when completed it will have capacity for 13,000 faithful and is, in medieval fashion, a work of storytelling art, rich in iconography and symbolism, at once ancient and thoroughly modern. (www.sagradafamilia.cat; Carrer de Mallorca 401; adult/child under 11yr €14.80/free; ⊙9am-8pm Apr-Sep, to 6pm Oct-Mar; Ⓜ Sagrada Família)

🍴 **Michael Collins Pub** (Plaça de la Sagrada Família 4) is an unusually authentic Irish pub, frequented by locals.

MORNING

From ❶ to your afternoon destination

🚶 🚶 🚶 🚶 🚶 🚌 🚶 🚶 🚶 Ⓜ 🚶 Ⓜ 🚌
35min 15min 15min 10min 10min 30min 15min 10min 5min 25min 30min 20min 50min

Completed in 1914 with a Modernisme-influenced design, this is one Barcelona landmark where the architecture is overshadowed by what lies within – the freshest produce from around Spain, the evocative starting point of many a memorable Barcelona meal, and a hum of activity unlike anywhere else in the city. (www.boqueria.info; La Rambla 91; ⊙8am-8.30pm Mon-Sat; Ⓜ Liceu)

★ **Top tip** Many stalls, including most of those selling fish, are closed on Mondays.

Mercat de la Boqueria
La Rambla
Liceu Ⓜ

🍴 For market-fresh food and some of the market's best cooking, pull up a stool at El Quim.

AFTERNOON

From ⓮ to your evening destination

🚶 🚶 🚶 🚶 🚶 🚶 🚶 🚶 🚶 Ⓜ 🚶 🚶
5min 10min 5min 25min 25min 5min 20min 5min 30min 15min 25min 5min 20min

Everyone walks La Rambla during a Barcelona stay. In just a 1.25km strip you'll encounter food stalls, flower stands, street performers, grand public buildings, a pungent produce market, pickpockets, prostitutes and a veritable United Nations of passers-by. More than anywhere else this is where the city's passion for life as performance finds daily expression, as a relentless tide of people courses down in a beguiling counterpoint to the static charms of Gaudí's architectural treasures. (Ⓜ Liceu)

★ **Top tip** Take an early morning stroll and another late at night to sample La Rambla's many moods.

Ⓜ Liceu
La Rambla

🍴 **Cafè de L'Òpera** (at no 74) has had a front-row seat on La Rambla since 1929 and is the perfect old-city rest stop.

EVENING

BEST OF
, QUICKLY.

+01; adult/c...
Apr-Sep, to 6pm

From **1** to

🏃 🏃 🏃
35min 15min 15min

Completed in
fluence

The transport planner shows you how long it takes to get from one activity to the next, by 🏃 foot, 🚌 bus, Ⓜ metro or 🚆 train.

Lice...

🍴 For market-fresh food and some of he market's best cookir ull up a stool at El Quir

🍴

Find the best and closest eating options to where you're enjoying your day.

..n 25min 5m...

Ⓜ Liceu

La Rambla ◎

Mini-maps help you get your bearings and show you the nearest transport stops.

Turn over for the fold-out map to help you plot your perfect day.

BARCELONA

PULL-OUT MAP AT BACK WITH TRANSIT MAP

Parc de la Collserola

(13)

TIBIDABO

Parc de la Creueta del Coll

VALLCARCA

Park Güell

(6)

EL CARMEL

(12)

SARRIÀ– SANT GERVASI

Jardins del Turó del Putget

SANT GERVASI DE CASSOLES

GRÀCIA

Parc de l'Oreneta

SANT GERVASI

SARRIÀ

(10)

PEDRALBES

L'ESQUERRA DE L'EIXAMPLE

Jardins del Palau de Pedralbes

ZONA UNIVERSITÀRIA

(39)

LES CORTS

SANTS

SANT ANTONI

COLLBLANC

LA TORRASSA

EL POBL SEC

(37)

(24)

(11)

(18)

Antic Jardí Botànic

Anella Olímpica

Jardí Botànic

Parc del Migdia

MONTJUÏC

LONELY PLANET'S
3 PERFECT DAYS

DAY 1

1 LA SAGRADA FAMÍLIA Beat the queues with an early visit to Barcelona's otherworldly standout sight.

14 MERCAT DE LA BOQUERIA Grab a market-fresh lunch and enjoy the hum of activity and colour.

33 TAPAS IN LA RIBERA Hit several of the city's liveliest tapas bars.

DAY 2

2 CASA BATLLÓ Start your day at one of the city's most beautiful buildings.

15 MUSEU PICASSO Spend a couple of hours at one of Barcelona's most rewarding museums.

31 GRAN TEATRE DEL LICEU Enjoy a spectacular night out at the grand old opera.

DAY 3

5 MUSEU D'ART CONTEMPORANI DE BARCELONA (MACBA) This captivating art centre will keep you busy for at least a couple of hours.

16 LA CATEDRAL Quietly contemplate the singular and monumental beauty.

27 LA RAMBLA Experience the city's passion for life.

1 LA SAGRADA FAMÍLIA

Gaudí's holy mission; a work of storytelling architecture

14 MERCAT DE LA BOQUERIA

The freshest produce from around Spain, and a hum of activity

27 LA RAMBLA

See the city's passion for life

A trip to the city's highest peak is an old-style family outing bursting with nostalgia. The panoramic vistas are themselves a fine reward and the amusement-park rides are a retro trip to fun parks of yore. One of the best parts of the experience is getting here: take the old tram that rattles along an avenue lined with Modernista mansions; then hop aboard the funicular for a speedy ascent to the top. (www.tibidabo.cat; R FGC train to Avinguda Tibidabo)

★ **Top tip** Ascend the old church or the new tower for even better views.

Gaze out over the city from balcony restaurant **Mirablau** (Plaça del Doctor Andreu, from 11am) on the way up to Tibidabo.

MORNING

From ⑬ to your afternoon destination

🚶 🚶 🚶 🚶 🚶 🚌 🚶 🚶 🚶 Ⓜ Ⓜ Ⓜ 🚌
20min 5min 30min 25min 20min 30min 30min 20min 20min 25min 25min 20min 50min

Both a pioneering Modernista building (completed in 1885) and the major collection of leading 20th-century Catalan artist Antoni Tàpies. Known for his esoteric work, Tàpies died in 2012, aged 88, leaving behind a powerful range of paintings and a foundation intended to promote contemporary artists. It's worth seeing the one-hour documentary on his life, on the top floor, to understand his influences, method and the course of his life. (www.fundaciotapies.org; Carrer d'Aragó 255; adult/concession €7/5.60; ◷10am-7pm Tue-Sun Ⓜ Passeig de Gràcia)

Choose from the abundance of tapas and *montaditos* (canapés) at **Cerveseria Catalana** (Carrer de Mallorca 236).

AFTERNOON

From ㉖ to your evening destination

Ⓜ 🚌 🚌 Ⓜ 🚌 🚌 🚌 🚌 Ⓜ Ⓜ 🚌 Ⓜ Ⓜ
30min 50min 45min 20min 50min 40min 50min 40min 40min 35min 35min 35min 25min

For the sports-minded, little can compete with the spectacle of a match at FC Barcelona's massive football stadium. With a loyal fan base and a gifted team, Camp Nou always hosts a good show – the stadium is well matched with the grandeur of the team's achievements, and attending a match amid the roar of the crowds is an unforgettable experience. Buy tickets online, or at FC Botiga shops and tourist offices. (www.fcbarcelona.com; Carrer d'Aristides Maillol; adult/child €23/17; ◷10am-7.30pm Mon-Sat, to 2.30pm Sun; Ⓜ Palau Reial)

★ **Top tip** There are plenty of scalpers selling tickets; make sure you're seated before paying.

A lively spot for tapas and a few beers, **Lizarran** is just outside Les Corts metro station.

EVENING

🚇 GETTING AROUND

METRO

The best way to get around Barcelona is the Metro. Trains run from 5am to midnight Sunday to Thursday and holidays, from 5am to 2am on Friday and days immediately preceding holidays, and 24 hours on Saturday.

Plan your journey at www.tmb.net.

Check out the Metro map on the pull-out map at the back of this book.

TARGETES

The cheapest way to use the metro (and most transport in Barcelona) is a targeta. Purchase your ticket at vending machines at all metro stations using cash or credit card. Targetes are multitrip transport tickets. The prices given here are for travel in Zone 1.

Targeta T-10 (€10.30) – 10 rides (each valid for 1¼ hours) on the metro, buses, FGC trains and rodalies. You can change between metro, FGC, rodalies and buses. Three-day tickets (€25.50) enable unlimited travel on all transport except the Aerobús.

HOW TO USE THE METRO

Colour-coded subway lines are named by letter or number, and most carry a collection of trains on each line, eg the red-coloured line in Manhattan is the 1-2-3 line. These trains follow roughly same path in Manhattan then branch out in the Bronx.

Beware of ...

Next stop, Manhattan? That really would make your day! This *How to Use the Metro* section is (mistakenly) about NYC. For more information on how to use the Barcelona Metro, visit www.tmb.net

... weekends. Lines are ... suspended. Be sure to check www.mta.info for weekend schedules.

FROM THE AIRPORT

BCN

17km southwest of central Barcelona

Ⓜ €4.10, 25 minutes

🚍 €5.90, 30 to 40 minutes

🚕 €25 to €30, 30 minutes

Train operator Renfe runs the R2 Nord line every half-hour from the airport (from 5.42am to 11.38pm) via several stops to Barcelona's main train station, Estació Sants (Plaça dels Països Catalans; Ⓜ Estació Sants), and Passeig de Gràcia in central Barcelona, after which it heads northwest out of the city.

The trip between the airport and Passeig de Gràcia takes 25 minutes. A one-way ticket costs €4.10.

The airport train station is about a five-minute walk from Terminal 2. Regular shuttle buses run from the station and Terminal 2 to Terminal 1 – allow an extra 15 to 20 minutes.

OTHER TRANSPORT

Great views. Normally operate between 5am and 11pm, but there are also many yellow *nitbusos* (night buses). Targetes can be used on the buses; a single ride costs €2.15.

Easy. Taxis charge €2.10 flag fall plus meter charges of €1.03 per kilometre (€1.30 from 8pm to 8am and all day on weekends). The trip from Estació Sants to Plaça de Catalunya, about 3km, costs about €11. You can flag a taxi down in the streets.

Pedal power. Over 180km of bike lanes have been laid out across the city, so it's possible to commute on two wheels. Try BarcelonaBiking.com (www.barcelonabiking.com; €2.15 per day) or Biciclot (bikinginbarcelona.net; €17 per day).

SHOPPING

SHOP FOR YOURSELF

Whatever you're shopping for, you'll quickly realise that Barcelona is a style city. An icon of the Barcelona design scene, Vinçon (Passeig de Gràcia 96, L'Eixample; pictured right) has the slickest

furniture and household goods. Everyone from Salvador Dalí to Jean Paul Gaultier has ordered a pair of espadrilles (the iconic Catalan ropesoled canvas shoes) from their birthplace, La Manual Alpargatera (Carrer d'Avinyó 7).

SHOP FOR OTHERS

Even the souvenirs in Barcelona have flair. Though primarily a store for smart homewares, Vinçon (Passeig de Gràcia 96, L'Eixample) also has a great range of Barcelona-themed gifts. La Rambla is packed with

souvenir hawkers; MACBA has an extensive bookshop which also sells quirky gifts and small design objects. At Cacao Sampaka (Carrer del Consell de Cent 292; pictured right), you can fill an elegant little gift box with chocolates in every conceivable flavour.

SHOP FOR KIDS

El Ingenio (Carrer d'en Rauric 6, Barri Gòtic) is a whimsical fantasty store where you can pick up a a flamenco costume or examples of the papier-mâché

models used in Catalan festivals. For paraphernalia pertaining to what many locals consider the greatest team in the world, without traipsing out to Camp Nou, visit the FC Botega store (Carrer de Jaume I 18) in Barri Gòti. Taller de Marionetas Travi (Carrer de n'Amargós 4) sells beautifully handcrafted marionettes.

NEED TO KNOW

MONEY

ATMs widespread. Credit cards also widely accepted.

TIPPING

Taxi Optional, but most locals round up to the nearest euro.

Restaurants Catalans typically leave 5% or less; leave more for great service.

USING A CREDIT CARD

When paying with a credit card, a photo ID is often required, even for chip cards where you're required to enter your PIN (for US travellers without chip cards, just indicate that you'll give a signature).

OPENING HOURS

Siesta Generally between 1pm and 4pm – many shops, businesses and some museums and art galleries are closed.

Museums & Galleries Many museums and art galleries are also closed all day on Monday and from 2pm on Sunday.

WEBSITES

Barcelona (www.bcn.cat/en) Town hall's official site with plenty of links.

Barcelona Turisme (www.barcelonaturisme.com) City's official tourism website.

Lonely Planet (www.lonelyplanet.com/spain/barcelona) Destination information, hotel bookings, traveller forum and more.

DOS & DON'TS

Barcelona is fairly relaxed when it comes to etiquette. A few basics:

Greetings Catalans, like other Spaniards, usually greet friends and strangers alike with a kiss on both cheeks, although two males rarely do this. Foreigners may be excused.

Visiting Churches It is considered disrespectful to visit churches as a tourist during Mass and other worship services. Taking photos at such times is a definite no-no.

Escalators Always stand on the right to let people pass, especially when using the metro.

ℹ️ IF YOU LIKE...

ANTONI GAUDÍ

Modernisme was personified by the visionary work of Antoni Gaudí, a giant in the world of architecture. **1** La Sagrada Família was his holy mission; **6** Park Güell, where he turned his hand to landscape gardening, is one of his best-loved creations; and **21** Palau Güell is a magnificent example of the early days of his fevered architectural imagination.

FREE STUFF

Many great museums have free entry after 3pm on Sundays and/or on the first Sunday of the month, including **7** Museu d'Història de Barcelona. Barcelona also has some stunning churches and other buildings that don't charge admission; arrive at **16** La Catedral at 8am to beat the crowds. People watching on **27** La Rambla is free and entertaining anytime!

FAMILY ACTIVITIES

Kids (and kids at heart) will be fascinated by the Amazon raiforest at **12** CosmoCaixa. Handsomely landscaped **23** Parc de la Ciutadella has a zoo, and you can hire a small rowing boat for a paddle on the lake. The whole family will find the atmosphere at an FC Barcelona match at **39** Camp Nou unforgettable.

BEHIND THE SCENES

SEND US YOUR FEEDBACK

We love to hear from travellers – your comments help make our books better. Visit lonelyplanet.com/contact to submit your updates and suggestions.

ACKNOWLEDGMENTS

Thanks to

Lonely Planet's Barcelona writers: Regis St Louis, Sally Davies, Andy Symington

Inhouse staff: Mark Adams, Cam Ashley, Sasha Baskett, Katie Coffee, Penny Cordner, Brendan Dempsey, Ryan Evans, Larissa Frost, Paul Harding, James Hardy, Anna Harris, Corey Hutchison, Andi Jones, Chris LeeAck, Georgina Leslie, Jodie Martire, Matthew McCroskey, Campbell McKenzie, Virginia Moreno, Wayne Murphy, Darren O'Connell, Naomi Parker, Piers Pickard, Martine Power, Samantha Russell-Tulip, Angela Tinson, Daniel Tucker, Tracy Whitmey

Images: ❶ Matt Munro/Lonely Planet ©; ❷ Manfred Gottschalk/Getty Images ©; ❸ Diego Lezama/Getty Images ©; ❹ Manfred Gottschalk/Getty Images ©; ❺ Exterior of MACBA (Musea d'Art Contemporani), Architect Richard Meier, Matt Munro/Lonely Planet ©; ❻ Manfred Gottschalk/Getty Images ©; ❼ age footstock/Robert Harding ©; ❽ Fabrizio Troiani/Alamy ©; ❾ Ken Welsh/Alamy ©; ❿ age fotostock/Alamy ©; ⓫ LOOK/Robert Harding ©; ⓬ provided by the Museum CosmoCaixa ©; ⓭ LOOK/Robert Harding ©; ⓮ M. Gebicki/Getty Images ©; ⓯ age fotostock/Robert Harding ©; ⓰ Manfred Gottschalk/Getty Images ©; ⓱ Allan Baxter/Getty Images ©; ⓲ Fundacio Joan Miro "Pair of lovers playing with almond blossoms. Model for the sculptural group at La Défense Paris 1975"/Getty Images ©; ⓳ Image Broker/Robert Harding ©; ⓴ JLImages/Alamy ©; ㉑ Randy Duchaine/Alamy ©; ㉒ Diego Lezama/Getty Images ©; ㉓ Jean-Pierre Lescourret/Getty Images ©; ㉔ Ingolf Pompe 52/Alamy ©; ㉕ age fotostock/Robert Harding ©; ㉖ Antoni Tàpies Núvol i cadira 1990 age footstock/Alamy © Fundació Antoni Tàpies 2014 ©; ㉗ Alex Segre/Alamy ©; ㉘ age fotostock/Alamy ©; ㉙ Niko Guido/Getty Images ©; ㉚ Matt Munro/Lonely Planet ©; ㉛ LOOK/Robert Harding ©; ㉜ LOOK Die Bildagentur der Fotografen GmbH/Alamy ©; ㉝ travelstock44/LOOK-foto/Getty Images ©; ㉞ LOOK/Robert Harding ©; ㉟ Quim Roser/Getty Images ©; ㊱ age fotostock/Alamy ©; ㊲ Steve Allen/Getty Images ©; ㊳ Ingolf Pompe 52/Alamy ©; ㊴ Lucas Vallecillos /Robert Harding ©; Getting Around (top to bottom): Kevin Foy/Alamy ©; Peter Erik Forsberg/Robert Harding ©; Shopping: Mark Avellino/Getty Images ©; Factoria Singular/Robert Harding ©; Lonely Planet/Getty Images ©; Peter Adams/Getty Images ©; Lonely Planet/Getty Images ©; Need to Know: Ursula Alter/Getty Images ©

Cover images: (top to bottom) La Pedrera, Russell Kord/Alamy ©; Park Güell, John Kellerman/Alamy ©; Palau Nacional, Juan Jose Pascual/Alamy ©

OUR STORY

A beat-up old car, a few dollars in the pocket and a sense of adventure. In 1972 that's all Tony and Maureen Wheeler needed for the trip of a lifetime – across Europe and Asia overland to Australia. It took several months, and at the end – broke but inspired – they sat at their kitchen table writing and stapling together their first travel guide, *Across Asia on the Cheap*. Within a week they'd sold 1500 copies. Lonely Planet was born. Today, Lonely Planet has offices in Melbourne, London and Oakland, with more than 600 staff and writers. We share Tony's belief that 'a great guidebook should do three things: inform, educate and amuse'.

GET THE RIGHT GUIDES FOR YOUR TRIP

CITY & COUNTRY
- The original
- Comprehensive
- Adventurous

DISCOVER
- Best-of
- Photo-packed
- Inspirational

POCKET
- Pocket-sized
- Easy-to-use
- Highlights

LOOKING FOR OTHER TRAVEL RESOURCES?

LONELYPLANET.COM
For travel information, advice, tips & digital chapters

EBOOKS
Guidebooks for your reader

lonelyplanet.com/ebooks

MAGAZINE
For travel stories, inspiration & ideas

lonelyplanet.com/magazine

STAY IN TOUCH

lonelyplanet.com/contact

AUSTRALIA Locked Bag 1, Footscray, Victoria 3011
📞 03 3379 8000 **FAX** 03 3379 8111

USA 150 Linden St, Oakland, CA 94607
📞 510 250 6400 **TOLL FREE** 800 275 8555 **FAX** 510 893 8572

UK Media Centre, 201 Wood Lane, London W12 7TQ
📞 020 8433 1333 **FAX** 020 8702 0112

twitter
.com/lonelyplanet

facebook
.com/lonelyplanet

lonelyplanet
.com/newsletter

Published by

Lonely Planet Publications Pty Ltd
ABN 36 005 607 983

90 Maribyrnong St, Footscray,
Victoria 3011, Australia

1st edition April 2015

© Lonely Planet 2015
Photographs © as indicated 2015

10 9 8 7 6 5 4 3 2 1

Printed in China